GURU WORSHIP

Interesting Observations of Why Business Gurus Keep Getting Richer and Transformational + Heart Centered + Spiritual Entrepreneurs (Like YOU) Are Going Broke...

By: Tiphanie Jamison VanDerLugt, Esq.

The Yay Me University ISBN:

ISBN-13: 978-0615994772

ISBN-10: 0615994776

For print or media interviews with Tiphanie please

contact: *Press@TheYayMeUniversity.com*

Tiphanie Jamison VanDerLugt

Telephone: 1 (760) 565-3106

Email: *Tiphanie@TheYayMeUniversity.com*

Table of Contents

Be Authentic
Just Do it Like Me +
It's Not Me It's You

In this business building and personal development space, there's a strange phenomenon happening. I call it **GURU WORSHIP**... So, being the academic I am, I thought it would be cool to do a little "research"... and so... these are the *Interesting Observations of the Madness that is Guru Worship.*

"Never forget that you are one of a kind. Never forget that if there weren't any need for you in all your uniqueness to be on this earth, you wouldn't be here in the first place. And never forget, no matter how overwhelming life's challenges and problems seem to be, that one person can make a difference in the world. In fact, it is always because of one person that all the changes that matter in the world come about. So be that one person. " -Richard Buckminster Fuller

Usually *Guru Worship* begins with the best of intentions. It starts out with having an idea, wanting to start or build your business. Since, we "need" information, the first place we go, is good ole Google. We start looking around for "ways to make money" or "build our business", "make money doing what I love", "get more clients", "grow our business", "passion into profits"... all of those "things".

Immediately, because Gurus have either been around for-ever, so they have an enormous amount of backlinks, (links back to their website), old articles with outdated info and/or are paying for advertising (most likely paying for advertising), they show up on the first page of Google.

You then go onto their websites and see "testimonials", not realizing, that if you just followed all of the testimoni-al breadcrumbs, you would find that they are all leaving testimonials for each other... i.e. are "in a mastermind" together, referral partners, joint venture partners, or are in some other way, *(NOT INDICATED on their sites)* - connected to each other; Sort of a spiritual pyramid scheme, more on that later.

Now, according to Richard Cialindi, the author of the "Bi-ble" of how to get people to do what you want, a book called _"Influence"_, you become, "influenced", by their "so-cial proof". LOL.

So, you get on their "list" and start receiving their emails. You dig a little further and see that they are connected to other "big dogs" and think, "ok, I MUST work with these people to have the level of success they're having." Now, while this is NOT true, you follow them, believing that if you just "invest" that you will become "one of them".

Being that you are committed to making this vision of your life and business work *(insert profitable)* and wisely understand that shortening the learning curve (for the things you think you don't know), saves you time, energy and money, you go all in… pocketbook and all!

This isn't a bad thing necessarily, well at least not in the beginning; but as I said, this is only the beginning.

So, the "investments" in courses/programs/products start to pile up. Whatever happened to leveraging someone else's experience and shortening the learning curve? You buy this program, that course, read this eBook, join networks; following each plan/program and training to the letter. In the end, the results are almost non-existent.

When you bring this to the program creator, you are told; it is your fault and about how all the other people are getting results in their businesses and lives. You think to yourself, "… well, maybe I could commit more…?"

The idea that you aren't committed to your dream, business, and vision strikes just the right cord, and in reaction to the seed of self-doubt the guru planted, you reaffirm your commitment to "going big"; and of course, invest at a "higher level" for guaranteed results. Your investment according to the Guru, demonstrates to the Universe/Goddess/God, that you are committed to your vision. Are you seeing this cycle?

When you are still not getting results it's the ole "it's not me, it's you" speech... what is this the dating game?

Have you ever taken a hard look at what this is costing you? **Revenue doesn't follow a guru it follows energy, value and action.**

Simply stated...

Revenue = Energy + Value + Action

ENERGY- the "Being-Ness" YOU BE AS YOU SHARE and GIVE value to those you contribute to. Your individual potency and capacity... your power to create infinite possibilities and transform the possibilities into opportunities...

"There are many who are living far below their possibilities because they are continually handing over their individualities to others. Do you want to be a power in the world? Then be yourself." -Ralph Waldo Trine

VALUE- I believe Jim Rohn put it best- "You don't get paid for the hour. You get paid for the value you bring to the hour." Value is the transformation brought about or facilitated by YOUR capacities and potencies—that come THROUGH your BEING-NESS.

"You can get everything in life you want if you will just

help enough other people get what they want." Zig Ziglar

ACTION-The process of doing your Being-Ness... MO-
TION... Movement... more than just thinking about the
"idea" of doing something... more than meditating. Being
in the MOVEMENT of your *BEING-NESS...* movement from
the freedom of your choice.

*"Action is a great restorer and builder of confidence. Inaction
is not only the result, but the cause, of fear. Perhaps the action
you take will be successful; perhaps different action or ad-
justments will have to follow. But any action is better than no
action at all." Norman Vincent Peale*

Interestingly, many of the female Gurus peddling "authentic marketing" and "proven systems" aren't taking your
EVA into account; seeking to turn you into **less successful versions of themselves.**

**Here is the thing... the world celebrates an original, not
the knock off.**

Thomas Carlyle says, "The merit of originality is not novel-
ty; it is sincerity". If the basis of originality is sincerity,
then how does one become sincere by trying to be like
someone else?

Which begs the question, if the goal is to be "authentic",
why are they not harnessing the power of your potencies
for YOUR revenue? Three of the more powerful female gurus in the "business coaching/lifestyle business" space

come from loving families, heck one was raised in one of the most affluent states in the United States. Now, while I would never suggest that where you are, is where you have to remain-- rather than trying to make you a version of her (which is a total set up for failure) and calling it "authentic"; take your potencies (i.e. experiences, background, obstacle overcoming spirit) and help turn that into cash baby! YAY!

Consider this-- Do you think, as a preacher's kid, I didn't learn how to "read" and connect with people? I didn't come from a loving home or grow up feeling loved (or wanted). My view of the world is quite different from someone who did, see? A person coming from a loving home, knowing that no matter what, they will be loved, cared for and have a safe place to fall, is coming from an entirely different place, than someone who has gone from surviving to thriving, right?

What happens is, Gurus want to dress that up (sometimes literally) in a glamour, feel good, law of attraction wrapper, all in the name of "doing business authentically". There are even special words used, like, "marketing authentically", transparency and vulnerability.

Telling someone with low self-esteem and no support to just "live your passion", "be more committed", pick your niche, focus on your target market and client and money will fall from the sky. What is does that have to do with being original and/or sincere? Wait, seriously?

How about, hey, take all of that hustle, pain, savvy, and survival and translate those skills into cash- i.e. a solution buyers are knocking down the door to buy. For example, take a look at how someone survives abuse, poverty, being on the streets, neglect, etc.

Maybe you learned how to read body language, how to sell someone on your idea (without them knowing), how to hustle and create income (legally) where there wasn't one. Maybe as a single mother, you learned how to make $40 bucks, feed a family of 5 for a week- you know how the song goes- "how to make a dollar out of 15 cents..."

Instead of "find a niche", how about you go a little deeper Guru? Especially we some people are paying $12,000. Don't give someone your script, your copywriter and your cliché title and call it "authentic." The struggle to hustle is something very real and it is a potency. #YAYPOTENCY

More than choosing a niche, those potencies solve real problems- and guess what? For the record, niches don't buy, buyers do. Buyers pay to have a problem solved or at least 70% of them do. From a CEO to a new start up-- who couldn't benefit from learning how to budget, how to read body language, be more persuasive, and/or how to get high value for low cost?

Diving a little deeper into EVA...

Are you someone or do you know someone who has "rebranded" a few times? Or is in a constant state of "rebrand"? Have you ever noticed how the site and graphics change based upon the new mentor or guru? The guru who is going to "save the day", with their "no b.s." real talk? Heck, how many times, have your heard that line? It's like "no b.s." has become the new "b.s", but I digress.

Now, certainly, this isn't about the evolution and/or evolution of your business; Certainly, as you grow so does your baby (insert business), right? However, a yearly or sometimes bi-yearly rebrand is quite different than growth and evolution. Heck the word "RE" by definition means to "do again". Merriam Websters' dictionary states, "Re- a prefix, occurring originally in loanwords from Latin, used with the meaning "again" or "again and again" to indicate repetition, or with the meaning "back" or "backward" to indicate withdrawal or backward motion"[1]

Here is the thing though, if you began with YOU, and YOUR EVA, then you would simply be stepping into more of who you BE, rather than constantly trying to figure out who you are. For me, I say YAY, who I BE is YAY, for the next 30 years, I want to share the YAY. YAY is true for me. I didn't need someone to brand me as YAY. LOL

If you are constantly going backward, then how can you possibly be moving closer to your dream business?

Gurus tell you to place your hand over your heart in a glamour photo shoot, or to dance, and somehow that is supposed to represent being "authentic"? Or, they send you to one of their inner circle graphic artists, who (incidentally) designed their website and graphics and now you're "authentic"?

Howard Schultz, founder of Starbucks says it so eloquently,

"In this ever-changing society, the most powerful and enduring brands are built from the heart. They are real and sustainable. Their foundations are stronger because they are built with the strength of the human spirit, not an ad campaign. The companies that are lasting are those that are authentic."

How do you build something magical from someone else's heart?

Almost all absurdity of conduct arises from the imitation of those whom we cannot resemble." Samuel Johnson

See, the thing is, if any area of your EVA is disrupted, constricted, limited, judged, so is your revenue? Revenue or Guru, choose???

Sounds more like.... ***"Be Authentic, Just Do it Like Me"***

The Shame Mastery Cycle

Does this feel (sound) familiar?

After a big money production live stream, video presentation or some other "event", they sell you the next $1997 program and BECAUSE they reward action takers; they offer a 2 or 3 pay option plus some recycled bonuses. You dive into the program, because you are convinced that this is the way to get your "gifts" out into the world, build a business around your passions and make some serious money. Only to find, that most of the information in the paid course is a recycled version of the free intro training offered at the big money production with just some worksheets. Heck, it may be that your own notes from the free stuff were more thorough than the worksheets.

You hand over more of your money (again) and when it isn't working, despite following everything to the letter, you are met with the tried and true law of attraction response- i.e. "The product/program/coaching isn't working for you because you aren't thinking positively enough or you don't have the right "success mindset"; the obvious focus here on making you wrong, rather than addressing the inadequacies of their outdated "proven" system. It's a total set-up, right? If your lack of faith is causing their program/system/coaching or product to fail, then every question you have can be thrown back in your face—it's the old "it's not me it's you". How do you argue against that? Being that your confidence is a bit shaky, you start thinking, well, maybe it is me???

It's not like the guru says, "here is an outline, let's tailor it to get maximum use for your business…" but more like, "if my generic guru system isn't working it's because you suck and aren't spiritual…" God forbid, the lack of results despite your continued efforts, be the result of the quality and/or depth (lack of) of the program/coaching/product; that would be like sacrilegious right?

Can you say "Mini-Me"? Are they trying to make little clones? Excuse me, "authentic clones"…? Always remember, your revenue doesn't follow a guru but your EVA.

I call this the **Shame Mastery Cycle**- i.e. -When a guru activates shame in you so you hand over your power to them to keep you buying from them (and whoever they promote) and/or guilt you into thinking something is wrong with you because you didn't blindly buy on the spot.

As an academic, education and I have are absolutely smitten with each other. However, education without action is just a waste of your money and self-esteem. Meditation is great, but motion will beat meditation any day of the week. When you are caught in *Guru Worship*, education is overvalued and action is undervalued. Albert Einstein said it best, "Nothing happens until something moves." Movement towards the paypal button for another course from someone even when you didn't get amazing forward moving results is NOT action.

"Action is the real measure of intelligence." Napoleon Hill

Can Someone Say Spiritual Bait and Switch????

Is it just me....????

I have a first-hand account of one "Gurus" *flagship "how to build a successful business program"* that had more rules to it than when I took the California State Bar Exam.

Keep in mind this is a $2,000 program! I must say, it's one of the prettiest programs out there, but a business building program it is NOT. In fact, you would likely get more information just from free videos on YouTube; but of course most women think pretty equals money. LOL

Newsflash* it means money for her, NOT FOR YOU!

In this business building program (and I use "business building loosely" and many others like it, here is what happens-- You attempt to do business like the guru. Only, you don't have the gurus marketing budget, team, tools, ideas, contacts, support, or personality. Remember, always remember, the most vital piece of any service based business is YOU. More on that in a moment.

What's worse, is in the aforementioned program- what was sold as live "coaching calls", were less than that. Some of the rules for the "coaching calls" were outrageous! For the record, NONE of these rules are listed on the flashy, beautifully styled and written sales page:

1. Guru cuts you off if you talk

2. You must ask a question right away

3. Questions are relegated to a minute of

4. No personalized advice

5. You may not ask "self- serving questions" (i.e. about your situation)

6. You may not ask about your business specifically

7. You can only ask questions that other people can also benefit from

8. You may NOT send in your questions ahead of time, so that they may be addressed in the "coaching calls".

Some other experiences involved, things like:

➢ if you ask for some kind of depth, she brushes you off

- ➢ there is no conversation with her as such

- ➢ it's a one way (question) and response (generic blah blah, no targeted advice)

- ➢ sometimes you are instructed to watch old youtube videos the guru put out years ago to address a question in a paid

- ➢ if you ask her about how she does things herself, you get the brush... don't want to give the deets on how she built her own business nothing on things like affiliate marketing, PR, ad words, etc.)

- ➢ no up to date business or marketing advice whatsoever; more theory stuff

- ➢ you're left with a generic answer (not so much coaching in there)

- ➢ doesn't explain specifically how to make money or start a "REAL" and serious business...

- ➢ doesn't speak specifically of how she became or achieved guru status...

Can you imagine paying $2,000 for that??? Why not put those "rules" on the sales page or in the video? The Guru is claiming coaching calls with no coaching? Call it lectures, limited Q & A with a time limit, put up videos but don't call it coaching, please. It's less than honest, ah heck, it's a downright lie!

Why pretend prospects are getting access and business building tips when they aren't? Oh and if you check the fine print of the terms and conditions page, it says, "all sales are final and/or each refund request is evaluated on an individual basis."

Things that make you go hmmmmm?????

Side note: This guru is one of the "sweet ones", considered well liked and "nice".

I wish this was in isolation, but sadly it isn't. Even worse, it seems that women are more susceptible to these bait and switch shenanigans.

As for those "high ticket intensives", dare I go there? Hell, why not... Oh my gosh.

I can personally attest to one of my clients paying over $50,000 for 2 "high end masterminds" after being told by a female guru, "if you want people to invest in you for high ticket products/services/programs, you have to invest in yourself through the mastermind". Keep in mind, this is a "big name guru" that didn't give her the time of day at one of her big events.

Well, you know how it goes, if you hear bogus, bad ideas long enough, it becomes the industry standard and "truth".

Wait, HUH?

Do we tell a doctor who specializes in Oncology that she has to have cancer and survive it before she can serve other cancer patients? What about the fertility doctor who helps women conceive? Heck no. I know, I didn't need a lawyer before I became one, so should I not have taken high paying clients or marketed myself?

This is utter nonsense. Five things to consider:

1. You have to start somewhere. They tell you, not to work for free... they tell you, to own your value. They tell you to believe that you are worth the big money, right? How many times have you heard a guru talk about mindset, knowing your value and belief? Are you buying a mindset by "investing" $40,000+ in their high-end mastermind? I can think of more ways to generate motivation, if that is the idea... If it starts with mindset and belief, then I can BELIEVE without investing in THEIR program, no?

2. Investment in yourself, can take many forms. I spent upwards of $100,000 for my legal education. Does that investment not count?

3. No guru should hold themselves out as the second coming- selling and promising one thing and then delivering something entirely different in the name of "investing in yourself"; Remember *"A teacher's purpose is not to create students in his own image, but*

> *to develop students who can create their own image."*
> *~Author Unknown*

4. Investment can take the form of time; it's the most expensive, because time YOU NEVER get back... but at least it's honest; and

5. There should be a return on your investment, more than just "I get to play in your guru playground..."; and by play, I mean watch from the periphery, not actually "be in the land of the gurus".

The "bible" of building a business- "<u>Think and Grow Rich</u>", by Napoleon Hill speaks to this wild notion of money creating money...

> *"Some people foolishly believe that only MONEY can make money. This is not true! DESIRE, transmuted into its monetary equivalent, through the principles laid down here, is the agency through which money is "made." Money, of itself, is nothing but inert matter. It cannot move, think, or talk, but it can "hear" when a man who DESIRES it, calls it to come!"*
> *Napoleon Hill*

Things that make you go hmmmm......

Check this out- investment is defined as "the action or process of investing money for profit or material result." If you are paying $5,000 dollars (or more) for a VIP day, you want to be able to see in dollars and cents the lifetime value to your bottom line, of that money invested; more than just "I get to take a photo with you and put it on my website for social proof." Touching the "hem" of the guru is NOT my idea of a good return on investment. For a funny video about "touching the hem" and what some Gurus really think,

http://www.youtube.com/watch?v=-9yu7HF8j4E#t=130

In other words, the value should outweigh investment, or else don't call it that.

Now... here is one for the ages....

So you are invited *(insert lured)* to attend a "live event" with a cool title, by a guru; you know, something low cost... maybe $97 bucks or less. Of course, in their promo video, email, or post on facebook, they promise to tell you all the steps to, get more clients, attract money, monetize your message, passion into profits, get a cash infusion, or something of that ilk; just pick just about any title, with the usual cool buzzwords, right? Hell, they may even offer a bring a friend for free ticket.

You sign up and maybe even bring a friend. More than the $97 bucks + parking, food, and other travel expenses, you offer the guru, the most valuable thing on earth, YOUR TIME- since you never get your time back.

The "live event" is for an evening or maybe an entire day; Most of which is spent on "mindset", right? The mindset of successful people, the mindset of an entrepreneur, the mindset of millionaires and on and on; at least two-thirds of "event" is spent on mindset- i.e. be more positive, positive belief, do the inner work, clean your desk to be clutter free, blah blah blah.

This is not to suggest that mindset isn't important. In fact, I recognize that in order to create anything magical, you have to first BE that magic. However, I don't personally subscribe to the idea that there is one "Success Mindset". For more on that, check out, my book http://theradicalselfexpert.com/

Any who, after droning on about how much she "loves" everyone in the audience and wants everyone to succeed...and, of course, after the parade of "success stories" across the stage, she proceeds to give what you think is actual content. By content, I mean, REAL TOOLS and STEPS to move your business forward. Or at least you think you are going to get some real tools. After all, in the promo "stuff", promises were made, right? You were told that showing up to this event would be life changing and your business would never be the same.

As you excitedly anticipate these awesome steps to change your business and life, you are given a brief overview of the steps required; only it's little more (or not) of what she has already offered in her weekly blog posts or videos. She further tells you the importance of each and every step, how you absolutely can NOT move forward without all of the steps. Also, you probably hear things like, "No one else is teaching this stuff..." or "I am going to do something crazy here and give a fast action discount"... or "I can't believe I am telling you this..." or "I wish I had known this when I was starting... " or "I am just like you... I know how you feel"... or "this is no fluff stuff"... Haha... Sound familiar?

Here is the kicker.... To get the deets of these ALL important steps (that ONLY SHE IS TEACHING), you have to come to a higher priced event in another geographical location, typically nowhere NEAR YOUR HOME. Ever graceful and condescending, she offers to discount the higher priced event for all of those in attendance; oh and by higher priced, I am talking 20+ times the cost of lower priced event you were already attending!

WAIT.... HUH?????

You've been had, hoodwinked, bamboozled, led astray, run amuck....

Can you say Spiritual Bait and Switch...????

Yes, motivation is great, but I can get that from Oprah's Lifeclass. Besides, that is NOT what was sold to you. You weren't sold, show up to this "Monetize Your Message/Passion to Profits event" to get "motivated". You showed up thinking you would get awesome real time content that would move your life and biz to the next level. Passion is great, but profits, well, that's a game changer, no?

I am sure if we went through those old sales pages, promo emails and such, there would be little to NOTHING about being motivated, right?

Intellectual + Creative Stifling/ True Self Suppression

Guru Worship creates an intellectual and creative laziness *(insert dependence)* at its best. At its worst, it is a complete suppression of your unique truth.

Rather than taking action on your unique insight or brilliance, you wait to get the seal of approval from your Guru. In reality, many gurus ARE NOT doing their own traffic generation, back- linking, video optimization, Seo or content product creation. More on that to come…

Business is an ever evolving "space". Many gurus' businesses are built on what they did- NOT what they are doing today. So here you are with a 2014 business using 2009 "tools" and are puzzled as to why your millions aren't rolling in. In the age of information at your fingertips, put up a squeeze page and offer an "ethical bribe" just isn't going to cut it.

There are these "ideas" *(insert lies)* in business theory, that to be successful, you go and reproduce what was successful in the past. This is what the gurus are banking on.

Wait, huh?

So today we go to events (virtual or live), and are instructed to follow those success stories of yester year??? Remember, if something is said long enough, even if it's bogus and irrational, it will become "truth" and the industry standard. Chances are, if it worked in 2009, it won't likely work today. Heck, in 2009 there were no pinterest, no vines, snapchats, instagram, Google plus, Google hangouts, or at least they weren't mainstream. Just because they (the gurus) were successful back then, doesn't mean they would be successful today if they had to start right now, with nothing; and by nothing, I mean, no list, no team, no contacts, no joint ventures, no testimonials... just a vision and a dream, just like the rest of us.

When all think alike, then no one is thinking. Walter Lippman

Right now, I bet there are at least 10 things or ways, you have thought about getting your gifts, talents and knowledge out into the world + making money, but haven't done so; likely, because it wasn't in one of the courses, a guru said "it doesn't work" that way... or because it wasn't labeled by the "mentor" or coach as "authentic" or the "norm"...

When you are more concerned with Guru Worship, and following their "rules" and getting everything "right", you stop the flow of revenue. How many times, have you been caught up in the overthinking process? You know that cycle of education being over valued and action being undervalued? Maybe you are always looking for the rules of "branding" or the steps for discovery sessions that convert properly. You have a squeeze page up, but your funnel isn't making sense? You have cool names for your blog to be "*cute and clever*" but they aren't optimize to drive traffic for the search engines... the list is endless.

Don't get me wrong, as I said, I LOVE education, perhaps too much (if there is such a thing). However, just as important as education is taking action on that education. Remember the hot and wise (may he rest in peace) Bruce Lee said ... "Absorb what is useful, discard what is not, ADD What is UNIQUELY YOUR OWN."

Check this out....

Have you noticed that many gurus sound the same; Maybe a different package, but basically rehashed info? I'm sure you have encountered the same buzz words- "Success Mindset"", "Ideal clients", "Authentic Marketing", "Intuitive Business", "Client Attraction System", "Client Magnet", "Magnetic Marketing" "Purpose Diva" "Money Diva" "Money Coach", "Money Mentor" "Business Strategist", "Business Catalyst", "Brand Strategist", "Life Stylist", "Success Coach", "Sales Queen"... and on and on and on...

Have you also noticed that after taking a business course, the graduates seem less like themselves and more like guru clones? Oh they are smiling and happy but have you been to some of those Facebook groups? Jeepers, it's like the graduates are peddling the wares trying to sell their "stuff" to each other. It's quite sad really...perhaps in a desperate attempt to recoup the money they paid for the program??? Let's just say, the exaggeration of actual success is in NO SHORT SUPPLY, if you catch my meaning...

Things that make you go hmmm...

Step-by Step??? Can Someone Say... "Holding Out"...

I am sure you may have noticed this... but heck, it's worth a mention.

Take a sales page of just about any *"build your business"* guru program. Look carefully at the "modules" and or "curriculum". Are the tactics they used to get you to their course or program listed as a module??? I know I personally do a section on affiliate programs and unique ways to drive traffic in the **YAY Me Money Makers Blueprint.**

http://yaymemoneymaker.com/

Makes you go hmmm, right?

Consider this, many of the gurus are NOT writing their own content, driving their own traffic and/or doing their own link building, or video optimizing. How the heck would they know if something is proven or not in **_today's market_**? Do they base this on how many eager unassuming people buy their product?

Most of the information is like, pick a niche, set up a website, squeeze page, write articles, blog, guest blog, blah, blah, blah. Now, I just gave you- business building circa 2003. How could I in good conscience charge $2,000 bucks for that? Is that how they GOT YOU to their squeeze page? Probably not, they're running ads, using JVS, affiliates, ad swaps, reciprocal mailings, etc.

A large portion of building a successful business, is having YOUR OWN affiliate program. Go through many of the gurus "business programs". How many are giving you step by step information on how to build your own affiliate program? More curiously, why are they NOT teaching that as part of the business training, since they used an affiliate program to get you in the door in the first place?

One guru tells you to get close to a guru by buying their product. Then over time, they will want to cross promote you. Seriously? On what planet is this true? People go to the events and are paying top dollar for the VIP seats and can't get any time alone with the guru... seriously? How about instead of paying for another program you don't likely need, you use that money and buy some Facebook or retargeting ads? Heck, did you know you could get highly targeted ads on YouTube? Even still, you could reach out to YouTube channels with a lot of subscribers and followers and pay them to put a link to your product.

Does anyone ever question this???

Is it just me, or do these things all seem designed to specifically keep you spending more money and spinning more wheels, spiraling downward into a sea of self-doubt and confusion, so you buy another course / product / program / training???

I have heard the gurus (a list, b list, c list and d list) are one big "incestuous group of marketing hype." Give a listen to a video here... Now, this is a marketer who is in a mastermind, of one of sales queens...

http://www.youtube.com/watch?v=SYhivJdV6ts

This was something, I fortunately learned from day one.

Perhaps it was the fact that I was raised by "hustlers" in the business of religion, I came with a bit more suspicion than most. LOL- Well, that, and the fact, that I am a lawyer and have ALWAYS been an entrepreneur.

When I started reading and researching, I was noticing that the same people were giving testimonials on each other's pages, and on each other's tele-summits, each other's stages.

Even Stevie Wonder could see and put those pieces together. They are all in each other's masterminds, buying each other's products and services, essentially, sharing the same $100 bucks (if you will) so they can all say, they are making money. The guru in the middle, is leading the charge and using the power of peer pressure (yes, it exists in adults) to keep people in their high end programs despite people not making money or not being able to afford it (because it didn't live up to the hype).

They make you almost dependent on the group, feeding insecurity and self-doubt and lining their pockets. Can you say pyramid scheme? I guess if you use the words, "*authentic and goddess,*" then it's not so much MLM and more MLM light? This is not knocking MLM, but call it what it is, you know?

In the interest of time and length, these are but a FEW observations of Guru Worship. If you made it this far, YAY!

Take-a-YAYS
(Takeaway + YAY)

There are some important *Take-a-YAYs* from Guru Worship:

1. DON'T! Haha... in the words of the handsome and wise Bruce Lee (may he rest in peace-) "Absorb what is useful, discard what is not, Add what is uniquely your own." Bruce Lee

2. Guru vs. Revenue Choose. Remember: Revenue follows **YOUR** EVA- Energy+ Value +Action...

3. In the words of Jenny in Forrest Gump.... RUN FORREST RUN!!! If any guru tries to convince you that their way is the only way to be successful, Run... RUN LIKE THE WIN! No matter how pretty the website, no matter how cool, beautiful or "nice" they seem- RUN! She/he wants your wallet and worship, not your success and friendship. "A teacher is one who makes himself progressively unnecessary." ~Thomas Carruthers

4. "When you're pressed **(insert pressure)** to "invest at a higher level", remember, **if you can't make it**

work with a little money, it's unlikely you will make it with a lot. If the guru's course didn't move the needle in your life and/or business, then a higher priced one won't likely work either. Investing at a higher level, when the initial "level" wasn't fruitful is more about their ego.

5. Ask yourself before you invest, "Does the guru program require the use of their recommended tools?" Those extraneous tools have a cost involved as well. Is the guru offering those extraneous tools as alternatives to, or are they a requirement for "success". Do those tools involve using the service of one of their former students, friends, inner circle members, etc.? Are you feeling pressured to use those tools?

6. Other than feeling motivated, did the guru in his/her launch, email sequence, video, do more than inspire? Were there actual actionable steps you could take immediately; nuggets that go BEYOND what has been offered in their free training? Was the entire conversation or presentation about "inner" work and saying YES to yourself? Was it a parade of success stories? You can't build your life and business on someone else's success stories or meditation. Remember Einstein said it best, "Nothing happens until something MOVES".

7. Are you bargaining with yourself to justify invest-

ing in the program, product or service? If so, RUN FORREST! The return on invest should be obvious or pretty darn close.

8. Would you be cutting off parts of who you "BE" to use the "proven" system? I am not speaking to the "fears" of selling and all of that "stuff". [Remember I don't believe fear exists] Would you have to be less playful, blog when you hate to write? Network when you are an introvert? Are there alternatives to the things you despise to accomplish the results you seek? Would your core competencies have to be sacrificed to make this thing work?

9. Do you in any way feel "wrong"? Are you feeling contracted? Are you feeling heavy when you discuss your business vision with the coach / mentor???

10. Is everyone in the "inner circle" buying from each other? Are they passing around the same 100 bucks??? Are they asking you to pay for things that you could do for yourself, outsource with your people for a much lower costs in the name of value and quality?

11. Does the program or service include those tools and techniques they used to get you in the door? Do you get the feeling they are holding back (holding out the goods)?

12. Are you getting partial information and asked for greater investment to get the "deep dive" into a six figure or multiple six figure business?

Again, as I said, these are but a few of the interesting observations of Guru Worship... I know at some point, you have encountered one if not all of these observations. Remember to stand your ground, and know that YOU ARE THE KEY!

When in doubt, it's a simple question- Revenue vs. Guru....

I am a huge Ralph Waldo Emerson fan... he says:

"Insist on yourself; never imitate. Your own gift you can present every moment with the cumulative force of a whole life's cultivation; but of the adopted talent of another you have only an extemporaneous half possession. That which each can do best, none but his Maker can teach him." Ralph Waldo Emerson

Thank you for reading... for some life and business building resources, please come over to:

http://TheYayMeUniversity.com

Share the YAY... and share this book with your friends, family members... and heck, even your enemies. LOL

Warmly + YAY,

Tiphanie Jamison VanDerLugt, Esq.

About Me...

I am on a mission to infuse YAY energy into life and business helping success minded women + cool men break the rules and turn infinite possibilities into mind-blowing opportunities for more money, fun and freedom with ease while being true to themselves. Come on, doesn't that just make you want to say YAY?

The equation for me is a simple one-

True Self + True Wealth = Days Filled with YAY!=The Easy Way!

So, you know how solopreneuers, small business owners, service based businesses (lawyers, doctors, dentists...) and visionaries want to generate more income, but in a way that isn't sleazy and full of yuck, well, I help them create + expand multiple streams of levergeable, scalable win/win income with the secret of Y.A.Y. B.L.A.S.T.!

As a licensed attorney, life-long entrepreneur, trainer and World's #1 True Self for True Wealth Facilitator™, and founder of The YAY Me University, I invite you to go beyond the *"Self-Help Trifecta"* (i.e. The Positives, Knowing Your Big Why and Success Mindsets) into the space and limitless possibilities + opportunities of *Self-Expertise.* When YOU are a SELF-EXPERT, you save yourself time, energy, money and peace of mind, knowing what decisions to make and actions to take with ease.

I am the author of 3 books- the book, *The RADICAL Self-Expert, The Fastest Simplest 7 Step Method to Discover How to Be Your True Self, Change Your Life Now & Be Happy Today!~The Easy Way!,* which was #1 on Amazon Kindle for Self-Help/Self Esteem and #2 for Self-Help/Happiness is also the basis of The RADICAL Self-Expert Method, of which I am the creator.

Want Some More FREE Goodies??? Go to...

http://TheYayMeUniversity.com

http://TrueSelfTest.com

http://YAYMeMoneyMaker.com

http://TheRADICALSelfExpertMethod.com

http://TheBookontheTrueSelf.com

http://TheRADICALSelfExpert.com

http://TruetoSelfTest.com

FREE Biz Tools...

Guru Business Tools for Under $100.000

www.yaymemoneymaker.com/
GuruTools

Free Business Tools

http://www.yaymemoneymaker.com/FreeTools

---

[i]*The Merriam-Webster Dictionary*. Springfield, MA: Merriam-Webster, 2004. Print. And "Re-." *Dictionary.com*. Dictionary.com, n.d. Web. 22 Mar. 2014.

www.ingramcontent.com/pod-product-compliance
Lightning Source LLC
Chambersburg PA
CBHW071435200326
41520CB00014B/3710